Positively Poetic

Zowie Norris

ISBN: 9798398004892

DEDICATION

I dedicate this book to my wonderful family,
James, Phoebe, Jasmine and Dad, for being the inspiration
for many of my poems and musings, and for always being
there no matter what life has thrown at me, supporting me
and encouraging me to stay positive in your own unique
ways. Love you all.

CONTENTS

INTRODUCTION

The gift of poetry keeps on giving to me
Opening my eyes and my mind to see
The beauty of language, power of a word,
Gives me a voice-my thoughts to be heard.
It's both crystal waters and stormy sea
That's what poetry gives to me.

Z Norris

I've been writing poems for a long time – I have my parents and school to thank for that. As a child, I loved reading and loved learning new words, so when I found out that you can create rhymes, visuals and express emotions through poetry – I was in my element! Initially, I wrote them to inform and describe something, but as I have become older, they have been a great way to express my feelings and regulate my emotions with. Life can be wonderful but also very challenging and devastating at times, and reading and writing poetry has been so helpful to me. So, when the Pandemic took place in 2021, I

i

decided to publish my first children's book about having Hope – which was actually following a poem that I wrote at the time called 'Hope Rekindled". Following the success of this book, in 2021, I began sharing my poems publicly on my social media pages for the first time. The response that I received was so encouraging. It's so wonderful to feel that may poems are enjoyed and that many people can relate to them too. Many of the themes of my poems posted were around positivity, happiness and staying motivated, encouraging and practicing having a positive mindset, all building up to my first poetry anthology!

My poems are arranged under the following Positive Mindset themes:

1) Kindness and Positivity
2) Self-belief & Self-love
3) Following your dreams but being patient.
4) Resilience & Bravery
5) Happiness
6) Gratitude

I hope that you are able to find some poems that you can enjoy, relate to and that help you to think and approach different situations in life, with a more positive mindset too.

KINDNESS & POSITIVITY

KINDNESS IS NOT WHAT YOU DO, BUT WHO YOU ARE.

IF YOU ARE POSITIVE – YOU SMILE MORE AND ARE
OPEN TO A WORLD OF OPTIMISM AND HOPE.

What is love?

It's a connection, a spark -
In the daylight and the dark,
A burning deep inside.
It's real and raw,
An emotion you can't ignore
Feelings that cannot be denied.

It's passionate and calm,
Brings confidence and charm,
Endlessly honest but encouraging.
It's a serious laugh,
Along a steep and bumpy path,
A flower that's privately flourishing

It's elation and sorrow,
That's still there tomorrow.
Love is patiently demanding.
It waits for no one,
But aches when it's gone.
It's frustrated but understanding.

It's kind and always there,
To support you, help and care.
It blinds and can be irrational!
It can woo you-
It sees right through you,
Vowing to be unconditional

Bringing lows and highs,
Creating strong family ties
A connection with a soul mate.
Present in good days and bad-
But to have it - I am so glad!
As Love is truly … great!

Love is Colourful

Why should it really matter
If you love pink or blue?
Both colours are for everyone,
True colours shine from inside of you.

Why is it so important to
Fit in with the all the others?
When our bright and beautiful world
Is full of colourful sisters and brothers

Why should it be frowned upon
If you don't wear gender-related gear?
Colourful clothes cover bodies that's all,
Stand out with pride, don't live in fear.

Why is it an issue what pronoun you use?
You are you- individual and unique,
No other colour is quite the same
They may be beige- but you are teak!

Why should others judge you-
For who you are attracted to?
Isn't Love supposed to be blind anyway?
But it pulses through your veins so blue.

Why does society use colour to group people?
The colours of the rainbow, as bright as a star,
Remind us so brilliantly that love is love
So be proud of the colour you truly are.

Why should who you love,
Turn into someone's hate?
Love is a multi- coloured gift
It's too beautiful to discriminate!

So whatever colour you are,
Your feelings you shouldn't hide,
The world's palette is a wonderful mix
Paint your radiant rainbows with pride!

Smile and Wave!

Positivity- not everyone's a fan.
Toxic Tyron's truly can;
Anger the angelic and amazing,
Boss the bolshiness and bold,
Criticise the calmest, confident and clever.
Devastate the determined and driven,
Enrage the enthusiastic and empathetic,
Frighten the fearless and ferocious,
Goad the gentlest, genius
Harass the happiest and hardworking
Intimidate the independent idol,
Judder the justified and jealous,
Kickstart Karma, kill kindness,
Loose the love, louden the liar,
Madden the marvelous,
Niggle the nicest,
Overwhelm the optimist with their opinions,
Poison passion, pulling on power,
Quicken the quarrels,
Ridicule and raise and riotous reaction,
Shake the strongest, the special and skilled
Terrify the toughest and trained
Upset and undermine those who understand
Vex the victorious,
Weaken and worry the wisest,
Axe the xenophobic,
Yell at the youthful,
Zonk the zestful.

In these ways you're willed to react,
But stop - there is a better tact,
Remember it's your power they crave,
Breathe- you got this. Smile and wave!

If you are happy and you know it . . . I'm so glad!

Big eyes stare through to my soul,
Searching for acceptance and praise,
Searching for a smile, a purpose, a role
Searching through darkness for brighter days.

Relax child, stand tall child,
Have confidence, stay true,
Don't be so meek and mild!
There is no one like you!

Hard times don't last forever,
Some days are good, some days are bad!
It's ok to feel under the weather
But if your happy and you know it … I'm so glad!

Find something to be grateful for,
Do something just for yourself
Try to express your feelings more
Look after your mental health!

Always know how amazing you are
Unique and beautiful in many ways
If your life was an empty jar,
Fill it with love and happy days

Memories are bitter sweet

All my memories make me feel sadness
So don't try to tell me that
I have many reasons to feel happy and grateful
Because when all things are considered,
Memories are bittersweet
And I'm not going to hide my feelings by saying
The memories I have will comfort me
Instead, they will be a constant reminder
That my life is destroyed and miserable
And nothing you say will make me believe
I still can remember the happiness they brought
Regardless of what memory I have,
I am not positive enough to fully enjoy things
And I don't believe that
Happiness exists deep within me
Because whenever I look at my reflection, I always think
Am I as sad as people say?
Why are memories so bittersweet!

(Now read bottom up)

7

Mental Health Matters!

Your mental health and well-being,
Needs to be at peace and heathy
This is far more important
Than trying to be wealthy

There are always times
When we all need some space
To regain thoughts, self- regulate
Relax in our happy place.

There are some things
That we all can do,
So to help, I thought
I ought to name a few …

Exercise, combined with rest
Motivating you to do your best!
Drinking water- a balanced diet
Meditation ,(somewhere quiet!)
Listening to others, showing respect
Family, friends - let's connect!

Vital and supportive community care,
Knowing that someone will be there
To listen, reflect, evaluate, advise
Connecting with others is always wise.
Whether it's someone known or new,
When someone is actually there for you,

It builds confidence and self-esteem
Support each other- work as a team,
In such a rewarding and meaningful way
Strengthening communication every day,
Making resources, sharing a book,
There are some great stories-take a look.

Speak up, share any worries, please do,
I will listen - I'll be here for you,
There's happiness and less debate
When we all communicate
Connecting with others, as we should,
Results in your mental health being good!

Randomly Kind

A smile that warms the coldest heart,
A push to make an old car start.
Compliments creating a crimson blush
Removing time barriers that cause a rush.
Lending a listening ear to a lonely soul,
Washing-up everyone's breakfast bowl,
Hugging someone who looks upset,
Giving left over food to a person or pet.
Making a cup of tea - a lovely task,
Better when made , but you didn't ask
A tissue for tears or a runny nose,
Not stepping on someone else's toes
Covering when a team member is not there
Just showing that you really care!
Checking your neighbour is okay,
A free gift - on me - yes , please don't pay.
A note of thanks and appreciation
Looking at loved ones with adoration.
Asking someone how they are
Giving a lift to friends in your car.
Being happy for someone's achievement
Understanding and empathy in a bereavement
Contributing towards a charity
Clear fully providing further clarity
Making someone else's day
With the things you do and say
Do good for others and you will find
Randomly or returned - they will be so kind!

Mirror Your Expectations

You want happiness?
Smile and show gratitude.

You want to be loved?
Then embrace others too.

You want to be treated with kindness?
Be empathetic and supportive.

You want to be listened to?
Consider carefully the impact of words.

You want to be spoken to nicely?
Listen, be calm and polite in response

You want to be cared for?
Build meaningful relationships with others

You want to be respected by others?
Be consistent, honest and true.

You want to be treated well in life?
Mirror your expectations.

Beware of the Mumster!

A Sleep-deprived 'Mumster'
Is ready to roar!
Her angry red eyes
Are hard to ignore.
Her sleep has been attacked
By the time-sucking knight
Who's tongue lashing sword
Makes it so hard to fight.
She's hungry and tired
At the end of her tether
Her sunshine is affected
By new stormy weather.
If you dare to ask more of her,
You are risking your life,
The atmosphere around
Can be cut with a knife!
Proceed gently ,tread carefully,
Bring chocolate and tea!
Hugs and cuddles will help too
She's fragile, can't you see!
Rest and sleep will help her engage,
Without any prodding
Eyelids are closing
Her head is now nodding
As she slips off the unbalanced scale
Of her 'work life slide'
She's made it to Friday
Though sleep has been denied.
Coping mechanisms -to their limit are pushed!
Here's hoping this weekend
Is time that's not rushed!

Who's to Blame?

A victim of circumstance
Disregarded in one glance
Who never really stood a chance
Targeted to fail in their performance.

Any real and contextual information
Is deemed as 'excuses' by a nation
Who 'don't condone discrimination'
But 'react to' , not 'prevent' a situation

So when the changes take so long
Do we make the support more strong?
Or does the lashing of a tongue
Come to tell you where you've gone wrong?

Unfortunately it is the latter,
No further discussion on this matter!
Those high up , can't hear this chatter
Letting their minions take the batter!

Society needs someone to blame
When things don't work- they need a name
To call out and to label inadequate- lame
Someone to take the walk of shame

So let's try changing this situation
And listening to their information
Actually looking at the 'real' situation
Instead of damaging careers and reputation

Then those who may have lost their way
Feel supported and okay
They might actually decide to stay
In roles that they've lived night and day.

So next time when you read about
A person who has no clout
Don't blame, rant, scream and shout
Just stop a minute- hear me out…

There is always a back story
And someone ready to take the glory,
Life is not all 'Jack-a-nory'
Try telling them that you are sorry.

SELF-BELIEF & SELF LOVE

HAVING SELF-CONFIDENCE AND MOTIVATION,
EVEN IN CHALLENGING TIMES.

LEARNING TO LOVE YOURSELF AND CARE FOR
YOURSELF MORE.

Hope Rekindled

In my darkest days,
When your absence fills my body with pain
And despair.
When the toxic sting from a betrayal friendship
Fills me with negativity and doubt.
Feeling rejected and dismissed
Judged and scrutinised,
Ripping at my values, soul and self- confidence,

I stop.

I breathe in the air that keeps me alive,
I hug my babies that my heart beats for.
I kiss my soul mate, that makes me smile between
tears.
My father's arms bring care and comfort.
I dance to the rhythm and beauty of life.
Through the wild and stormy sea ,
Mighty waves and turbulent winds may have
knocked me off my feet, but I will not drown.
Strength and love help me to float.
Faith helps me to find a new shore.
My grateful heart beats to the rhythm of a story of
new hope.

Imposter Syndrome

What am I doing here?
Where am I going?
I don't know what I'm doing
And I've no way of knowing!

Who gave me these skills?
I can't remember learning
I feel so anxious, sweaty palms
And now my stomach's turning

I feel like such a fraud
Standing in this role today
Wishing that these doubts
And Worries would go away.

My achievements are not real to me
I must've had some luck that's good,
Please come back self- confidence
So I can believe in myself - like I should!

Stay Crazy!

You think I'm the one who's crazy
I must have 'Lost the plot'
Gone insane in the membrane
Well actually- I'm not!

I'm happy, I'm free
I have love in my life,
And a new chance to be me!
Really me - can't you see?

Over society's line,
I've stuck out my neck
Pass me all of my cards,
I'll shuffle my own damn deck!

I'm taking full control
It's scary- but quite fun
Just hand me a pen,
I don't need a gun!

Emotions flow freely,
Right through the ink,
Some stir a smile
Others make you sink,

To new a depth of despair,
Misery and woe,
But my crazy heart says
That's no place to go!

I'm cracking calm-fulness,
Resisting a reckless fight,
Using my voice, choosing my words,
Sharpening my sword to write.

Creatively staying crazy
Let's hit new madness heights,
But don't worry about me,
Just crazy Karma- she bites!

Your Health is Your Wealth

Can you hear my heart beating,
See life pulsing through this vein
Hear me inhale vital oxygen,
Shooting signals to my brain.

I can move, enjoy senses,
Beautiful earth - I can see!
I feel joy , happiness and love
And know there's only one me!

I can hear the sweet music
And dance my feet to its beat
Taste the delicious and divine,
Able to drink and to eat.

What I'm trying to say,
In my poem , bit by bit,
That your body is special,
So please look after it!

It's not about being slim or muscular,
Societies pressures can be unrealistic
Being well in mind and body,
Isn't about being aesthetic!

All the riches in the world,
Can be replaced - but not your health,
You can't work if your unwell either.
So your health - is your wealth!

Be kind to your body,
Eat, exercise hydrate and rest.
Combined with laughter and love.
It will function at its best.

Multicoloured Girl

Copper-streaked hair,
Glints and flickers like a flame,
Framing a porcelain face,
That cracks with an endless display of emotions.
Come and swim inside her ocean-blue eyes,
To see her reality,
Reflected on the mirrors to her soul.
A blood-red smile, reveals the pearly jewels,
Spreading sweet yellow vibes of joy.
Peachy skin that covers a multicolour of feelings,
Flowing through her body in crimson cells of gratefulness.
Her purple heart beats with passion,
Celebrating life's unique rhythm.
But inside her heart is a black hole -created since the loss
of her mother.
Strong pink love for her babies,
Keeps the heart pulsating.
Her rainbow soul creates strength and new hope,
So, she continues to paint the world with the colours of
her life.

Mermaid Pride

I want to be a mermaid,
To swim free under the sea,
Be loved and appreciated,
For being allowed to be me.

Life would be full of magic,
Colour, wonder and awe
Flipping my multicoloured tail,
At any worries I've had before.

I'm sure above the surface,
My appearance would be accepted
I'd have my own special category
That is adored and not rejected.

It wouldn't matter whom I loved,
Underneath or above this wave.
My unique beauty would be enough
To always be confident and brave.

Knowing how to weather a storm,
Swimming towards challenges with grace,
Riding the tides of life with many others,
But never feeling out of place.

To those mermaids on land,
Swim tall, do not feel denied.
Swish your rainbow tails,
With colourful mermaid pride.

Painted Smile

I'm going through the motions,
But don't really care to be near
Whether it's something I'm good at
Because I don't want to be here.
So you can look down your nose
Whisper behind my back,
Then pretend to be Friends,
If I've something that you lack.
It's a shame you feel this way
You're so pretty, you have style,
But your actions are so false
Behind your painted smile.
So pout those lips and strike a pose,
You're aiming for popularity and fame
Because your life's a competition,
And friendship is just a sad game.

Freak or Unique?

Society gives us labels,
Groups and gizmos,
Trends and league tables,
Popularities and political parties,
Hierarchies and heroes,
Famous and fiercest,
Wisest and wealthiest,
Sportiest and successful
Updated and additional categories create
New and unrealistic challenges for the young.

Youthful years spent desperately searching ...
Who are you? Who'll love you?
Where do you belong?
Social media seizes young souls,
Stealing time, Influencing thoughts
A zombified addict.
Squashing and squeezing out their self-confidence and
identity.
Succumbing to a virtual life.

Societies boundaries set the standards.
Cultural rules that seemingly justify cruelty...,
Virtual trends that encourage violence…
Limitations and expectations instruct on what to wear, say,
try, taste, befriend, unfriend, understand, believe and even
think?
Acceptance is the quest but is the desire of the prince of
princess to be rescued? Loved?
A surge of confidence, a moment of crazy defiance and
oppositional actions…
Break down bars constricting creativity.
Swim against the social-media current- dragging you along
the same lazy, hypnotic waters.

Intimidation from the popular ones may rear its ugly face.
Doubt and desire to fit in, seeps out of
pores created by hormonal growth.
Considered a 'freak' for being riotous
Only the strongest of nature
Would stand firm in their values and be unique.

FOLLOW YOUR DREAMS BUT BE PATIENT.

KEEP YOUR DREAMS ALIVE IN YOUR HEART AND YOUR MIND.

PATIENCE GIVES YOU A HEALTHY ATTITUDE TO BE CALM, ACCEPT AND GIVE YOUR BEST.

To My Younger Self...

Hey you! Always stay wild, bold and free
keep doing the things that bring you glee
Don't let other people take your control
Follow your heart - but protect your soul

Be passionate, stoke your fire inside
Don't hold back - you've nothing to hide
In your confidence- don't ever doubt
Your life's song should never fade out.

Give your attention to the things that matter
Follow your dreams- don't let them shatter
Don't give toxic people any of your time
Say 'no thanks' more - it's not a crime!

Stay kind not gullible - your instincts are right
Being made a scapegoat is just not right!
But allowing grudges just hurts you more
So, focus on the people whom you adore.

Appreciate all the little things
Until you smile and your heart sings
Love, explore, experience and learn
As so quickly does your lifetime turn!

New Beginnings

I'm feeling excited and nervous
To start again and somewhere new
But happy endings can sometimes
Need new beginnings - it's so true!

No matter what yesterday was like
Birds start a new day with a song
Dance to the rhythm of your own music,
Be brave, be true and stay strong.

With each and every glorious sunset ,
There is the chance for a new start,
Come rain or shine, no matter what weather,
You are the sky- just follow your heart.

Hard work and resilience is expected,
You can be deemed weak -not to stay
But a different strength needed
For knowing when to step away

So it's time to finish this chapter,
And begin writing my next book
Same passion flows out of a new pen
For my next adventure - wish me luck!

Positive Women Role Models

Women all around the world
We're thankful for you all today.
From little girls with big dreams
Fighting as women to have our say!

Within our feminine hearts,
Burns talent and creation,
Courageously braking barriers,
With pure positive, determination!

Working hard, running businesses,
Raising families ,achieving more than ever,
Multitasking to the maximum
Passionate in all that we endeavor

Over the years, standing up to be counted,
It's wonderful to think how far we've come
The responsibilities and rights of every,
Daughter, Sister, Aunt ,Nan and mum!

Ladies don't be controlled or told
That this is a man's world
As the song states- it would be nothing
Without a woman or a girl.

Thank you to all the women
Who's sunshine truly beams
For raising, loving and inspiring
Me to also follow my dreams.

Precious Time

Childhood memories- I laugh and cry,
As fun -filled time, soon flies by.

Teenage years -music fills my soul.
Time beats by with rock and roll!

Adulthood - the unbalanced time of work-life
I meet my soulmate and become their wife.

My children come and quickly grow,
I wish that time could now be slow!

So enjoy your time- dance in the rain
You'll never have time to do it again.

New Year - New Mission

Since the clocks have struck midnight
On the eve on the New Year,
'Driving home for Christmas'
Has just ramped up a gear!

Christmas is now over
The trimmings are all down
Back to school now girls
Upside down - turn that frown!

Resolutions made by many
To start, improve, do more
If not planned carefully
Soon become a chore!

Drink more water
Write another book
Read more, walk more
New recipes to cook

Tidy the house
Drink less wine
Come on keep up
You're doing just fine!

Back to work with a bang,
This week has been testing
My first mission this weekend
Is to do more resting!

Be patient- Rome wasn't built in a day!

Does time really stand still for you?
As it speeds by me with a jolt,
I have so many things to do
But they've suddenly come to a halt.

Why is it when you're so busy,
The inevitable takes place?
I thought I was good at multi-tasking
But now it's becoming a manic race!

So when will everything be achieved?
When will I fulfil my dream?
There are not enough hours in the day,
Things can't constantly sparkle and gleam.

Time takers come in different forms,
Priorities and values can sometimes clash
Taking you on a tangent of suggestions
Trying not to rush or do something rash.

The journey is testing but so worthwhile
Each step you make, be it big or small
Will bring you closer to achieving your goal
And patience is a virtue. after all!

Stop, rest, reflect and evaluate
Make tweaks and changes along the way
Life only has one real 'deadline'
Remember, Rome wasn't built in a day!

That Friday feeling

I'm tired but I'm happy,
It's Friday and I'm feeling fine
In my pyjamas by eight
Movie night and a glass of wine

Another busy week
With its highs and lows,
A non - stop pressure cooker
That's how work life goes.

But now it's the weekend
A time to relax and unwind
Time with family and friends
Rest my body and my mind

So cheers to Friday ,
The care free feeling that it brings
Have a great weekend everyone,
Full of your favourite things!

BE RESILIENT & BE BRAVE!

BEING ABLE TO WITHSTAND AND
RECOVER QUICKLY FROM DIFFICULT
CONDITIONS.

TAKE RISKS AND CHALLENGE YOURSELF
TO TRY NEW THINGS.

Keep Growing

Sow your

seeds of knowledge
Nurture them and show them love
Keep growing and branching out
Adding new leaves and flowers
With each twist and change
Don't stop,
Let your

mind   blossom
Listen and learn
To get

new shoots
Meet   people,
New

experiences,
First tastes,
Use all

sensations
Different

opinions
Cultures,

lifestyles,
Explore,

read,
Discover new places.
Never stop
Reaching
For the sun.

Just in Case!

My family always laugh at me,
Whenever we go anywhere
As I like to feel organised
Have some time to prepare

You may wonder what I'm doing
Or where my thoughts have gone to
I'm just going through the day ahead
Packing essentials and things to do.

Prepared for all kinds of weather
Additional clothes to those dressed
Too cold or too hot is not an option
And will result in us all getting stressed.

So yes I have more baggage
Please don't pull that face!
Yes we really need this
Not for now - but just in case!

Effortlessly Entitled

Nothing comes for free
Unless you're extremely lucky
Even then, luck doesn't last,
And life moves on too fast.

Truly blessed with a life and soul
Nourishing this should be your goal
The world doesn't owe you anything
Compose your own song to sing.

Hard work and effort is the price to pay
To be successful in your own way,
Real life does not entitle you to pass go
Money for nothing is just a game you know.

So appreciate all you have and do
Effortless entitled people may never queue,
Will they enjoy life's ride behind that pout
Or find something else to complain about?

Don't worry so much about the time spent
Enjoy life and be proud of any achievement
It's not a race or competition to live
Remember you always get what you give.

The Swan

Like a swan gracefully gliding
On a glittering lake,
Both slowly and steadily I swim
Along the twisting , testing
And turbulent waters of life
Remaining cool, calm and confident.
For all to see.
Beneath the surface of the water,
Is my anxiety, stress and hard work
Are paddling frantically
In a frenzy that only those close
Will know.
Other birds may assume I swim easily
Mistaking my graceful exterior
For arrogance- egotistical energy
But envy does not see reality,
Only the outer appearance facing them.

'Me time'

Waving at my complexion in the mirror,
We are alone again my friend
Silence surrounds me
My thoughts are on mute
But what can I now hear?
The sound of the birds singing outside,
A clock ticking on the mantelpiece
My heart beating, pulsing inside my ears.
Feeling forlorn, I stare at an empty room
But what can I now see?
Through the window, colour and beauty,
My cosy home, lived in and loved
Smiling and grateful is the woman in the mirror.
What is there to fear?
Socially missing out?
Gaining some 'me time'
Allowing my thoughts
To wander,
To think,
To ponder,
To feel,
To dream…
I'm no longer afraid
Time alone is essential.

Life is a Rollercoaster

I look in the mirror
But what do I see
Sometimes I don't recognise
The person staring back at me

Another day, another week,
Another month, another year
Is it time to make a change?
No! Shouts risk and fear.

Afraid to jump off the hamster wheel
Being dragged along with the crowd
Facing new challenges along the way
That do make me feel proud.

But don't ever get comfortable
Change is back to bite
This rollercoaster's about to turn
I'd better hold on tight.

To many changes can fling you off
But perhaps it's meant to be!
Just look out for where you land
Try to leave the ride naturally.

Sometimes change is out of your hands
But if you do what you've always done
You'll always get the same result
And the ride becomes less fun.

Holding new beginnings

Holding new beginnings
Standing at the end
Through tricky times , I'm still
Providing a helping hand to lend

Helping deal with life's challenges
It can get you feeling down
I bring out my best smile
When I'm trying not to frown

Memories spill from my eyes
When I look back over the year
Still proud of my achievements
Down my cheek trickles a tear.

New challenges and changes!
What will the future bring ?
To be optimistic and hopeful
Some say It's a great thing

(Now read from the bottom up
For a new viewpoint)

Loss

The day you left us,
My whole world changed
And it's never been the same.
Time moves on around me,
My family grow up in front of me
But you're not here to see this.
Why?
Some days I feel so angry and bitter
It eats me up inside .
The heavy weight of sorrow
Brings physical pain
But - the memories bring you back at night
As I lay in my bed, missing you.
They comfort me and bring me peace.
Heartache will be eternal
Like my love for you will remain strong.
I will miss you always.
Sorry but - I cannot move on.
Everywhere I see - reminds me of you
You'll live on in my mind and in my love for
My daughters- who adored you too.
For Love is a precious thing - it brings pure
Joy and elation to your life.
Sorrow and Grief also comes with love
And knocks you off your feet and leaves a scar that doesn't
fully heal.
So I'll smile at the memories and hold my children tighter
while I am able to.

Controlling My Destiny

I'm the author of my book
So I should own the pen,
To write all parts of my story
Writing new chapters again and again.

Better to be the pilot of my plane,
The destination should be no surprise
This way you can be readily see
Any turbulence that may arise.

For life is a testing journey,
Things happen out of the blue.
But experience makes you wise
To help you predict things too.

Not everything in life can be controlled,
But choosing happiness in what you do
Creates a destination of your choice
Killing karma and chaos - It's true!

So I'm choosing my destiny,
My life isn't anyone's game
If I don't roll my own dice
I may as well change my name.

Controversial Clarity

Some rules are meant to be broken
True words need to be spoken
Opinions need to be opposed
Love doesn't need to be proposed

Libraries can allow some noise
Girls can be stronger than boys
Some adults haven't been to school
Being smart can be considered cool

A clear plan with hidden agendas
Friends can be your next offenders
Can we agree to disagree …
Either with yourself or me ?

Sometimes your face doesn't fit
You can be attractive and not fit
At times, holidays can be stressful
Long journeys can be restful

A perfectionist can make a mistake
Some news can be true not fake
Arguments start when people agree
Life can be lived in a virtual reality

Faith can be had without praying
You can still be early when overlaying
Dismissing information that's been heard.
Controversially speaking without a word

HAPPINESS
AN EMOTIONAL STATE OF JOY, SATISFACTION,
CONTENTMENT AND FULFILMENT.

Summertime Song

Sing me the sweet song of summertime,
Full of melodies of joy and laughter,
Composed by loved ones and friends.
Freedom to daydream and create
Repeating favourite tunes again and again.

Head space to conduct and orchestrate,
No droning deadlines or screeching sounds,
No restrictive rhythms to a set routine
But time to explore new soundscapes
That paint warmth and happiness

Adventures played to your heart beat
Making musical memories along the way.
New Lyrics to be read and written,
To a relaxed and radiant tune, with
A beautiful baseline to bloom and grow.

Love your life

I came into the world
Forty six years today!
Apparently - born with a tan
In a heatwave in 76,
My birthday's in the sun began!

I embraced my 80's childhood
Crimped hair, fluorescent gear,
Matching with my little sis Kel,
Roller-skating, hanging upside down,
Scabby knees every time we fell!

My parents worked so hard,
And surrounded me with love
They ensured that life was great,
I loved my school and friends
Ange is still my best mate!

I never found things easy,
But was always encouraged to try,
As a child I always loved to read,
Lost and found myself in books,
Never knowing where it would lead.

Music , art and writing,
Is where I'm at my best,
A childhood dancing on stages,
Rocking out in a band at sixteen
Even singing at the first Oakwood beer fest!

I found love with James
After kissing a few frogs! (Ha!)
18 wonderful years of being his wife,
Became a mum to two daughters,
Then came the happiest times of my life.

My family is my world,
We've suffered a huge loss
But mum's laughter, love and fun,
Shines on through her grandchildren
Making amazing memories come rain or sun!

I've been an educator
Loved teaching many classes
Over twenty years - no resting
Loved working with the children
But Politics and pressures are testing

Writing is my latest passion
Complete with illustrations,
I'm proud to publish my first book,
Writing weekly poems too,
I've definitely got the writing hook!

Please don't get me wrong,
My life hasn't always been rosy
There's also been some great pain,
But if you love your life,
You'll learn to dance in the rain.

Motherhood

If I had all the riches in the world,
Fame, fortune and glory,
My life would be very different,
To my present, continuous story.
My time and reason I work so hard,
For my family, my life, my love, my team,
To provide for and teach them to
Always follow their dream.
Some may say I've got it wrong
But options- there was no other,
Some are able to stay at home,
But like many, I'm a working mother.
This doesn't mean I love them less
Not interested, or do not care
Our time together is always precious,
So many wonderful memories to share.
Since holding them as babies,
Their tiny fingers around mine curled,
I fell in love with them instantly
They're my everything - my world
I've enjoyed every step of their childhood
To the young ladies they have become
I'm the richest, happiness, luckiest woman,
Just being their doting mum!

Laughter is the best medicine

First, it's a snigger.
A grin stretches to a wide smile,
Wow, that felt good -
I haven't done that for a while!

A snort. A chuckle.
My cheeks are feeling flushed.
A burst of laughter -
I'm even getting shushed!

Sorry! I giggle in response,
I don't know what's come over me!
I've been very sad for so long
But this laughter brings me glee.

I can't stop- I'm hysterical,
The more you tell me to be quiet,
This emotion has been trapped inside,
It's coming out to start a riot!

My shoulders feel so loose and relaxed,
The stress is going away,
I'm crying with tears of joy
Hope this exhilarating feeling will stay.

Don't forget to breathe

Just stop what you're doing!
Hold it right there
Breathe In slowly
Inhale some fresh air

Don't panic - you've got this
Now exhale at your pace
Then repeat this action,
This isn't a race!

When life speeds up
You will need to slow down
Find joy and just breathe
It's too hard with a frown

Shut out the world
And count slowly to ten
Sucking oxygen in
Filling lungs again.

Gain composure
Shirk off the strife
Clear your head
Let the air bring you- life.

Flick kettle on

Who doesn't love a cup of tea?
My first and last drink of the day
So many different varieties
From peppermint to Earl Gray

For me it has to be Yorkshire tea
Or Tetley's - eye - it's rather nice
No sugar, but a drop of milk,
Stirred not shaken - to be precise!

A cuppa fixes everything
Helps you, when you're feeling blue
Warms your hands up in winter
Yet refreshing in summer too!

I'm a Yorkshire lass, I'll 'flick kettle on'
If you come and visit me ,
For a 'chinwag over a brew'
Dunking biscuits and pouring tea.

It's a great drink for socialising
A lovely term of endearment too,
Because when you're 'my cup of tea'
My feelings for you are pure and true.

Harpooning Happiness

Shake off sapping sadness
Fight off frustration and fear
Annihilate all anxieties
Wipe away that tear!

Find out what raises a smile
Put on your happy hat!
Harpoon your inner happiness
For what matters is just that!

For contented cheerfulness
Helps us mentally be okay,
A simple smile, a kind word,
Can made somebody's day.

So thanks to those in my life
Who make me laugh and smile
If happiness was something worn
It would be my chosen style.

The Past (A Haiku)

Don't dwell on the past,
Learn from it, and then move on.
It takes you nowhere.

Wonderful Weekend

Oh wonderful weekend
Glad to see you my friend,
To give me time to unwind
Some slumber time to lend.

Quality time with family
To talk, catch up and laugh
Loose myself inside a book,
Relax in a bubbly bath!

No schedules, deadlines,
No lists and tasks to tick
Time to think, to breathe
Just please don't go too quick!

Socially Switching Off!

Follow me - I'm popular!
Send me lots of likes
I don't know you- you don't know me
But let's hit new followers heights
I like your post you must be clever
You read many books
You only look 16 not 40
According to your looks!
What's my age and marital status
Got to do with my post!
No I'm not giving you my PayPal info
Oh your status wasn't meant to boast?!
So you like my picture
And want to meet up with me?
You didn't read my profile
I'm 'happily married' - you didn't see?!
Oh but in this world of pretence
You think it's still okay
To continue within your proposals,
Hoping they'll make me sway!
But hey - guess what - I'm real,
My social profile isn't just hype
And anyway- it's time to say...
I'm sorry love - you're not my type!

GRATITUDE

FOCUS ON WHAT'S GOOD IN LIFE AND BE
THANKFUL FOR THE THINGS WE HAVE.

An Attitude for Gratitude

So thankful for many a thing,
That triggers my smile,
Makes my heart sing
Brings joy and excitement
passion and zing!
An attitude of gratitude,
These feelings can bring.

Grateful for such a lot,
For the love from the present
And past- but not forgot.
For the cuddles when it's cold,
Beach days when it's hot,
Lessons learned when
Everything has 'gone to pot!'

I appreciate many things in life,
Fantastic friends and family,
Being a loving and devoted wife,
A proud mum of darling daughters,
learning from all troubles and strife,
The warmth brought from kindness,
Enjoyment, Excitement-just loving life!

Perfectly pleased for having time
Everyday routines and consistency
To the spontaneous and sublime,
For the raging seas to swim across,
Tall and treacherous mountains to climb.
For finding my voice deep inside me,
Spilling out emotions in words that rhyme.

Whatever life throws at me,
Whether fluffy, or explosive,
I'll embrace it or deal with it,
It's my book, my lesson , my gift,
I'm the writer of my own story,
My cup of life may not be fine China,
But it holds my precious Yorkshire tea.

Nature's Treasure

So grateful for our planet,
It's beauty and it's wonder,
The vast variety of species,
On land , in sea - on top and under.

The natural elements
Providing all our resources,
Stunning sandy beaches,
Mountains- including river sources.

Amazing Landscapes naturally formed,
That take your break away,
To man- made from earth's resources,
Constantly changing with every day.

As life on this planet has evolved,
We have used Earth so much more,
Chopping wood from the tallest tree,
Mining minerals above earth's core.

But now we need to limit,
Our use of earthly treasure
So that our children's future,
Will also have this pleasure.

This planet needs our help
Harm and destruction needs to quit
We're the only planet that's living
So let's all look after to it!

Real Superheroes

Superman flies off to save the world,
Spider-Man swings you off your feet
Batman is a mighty, caped crusader,
So many superheroes we'd love to meet.

Who comes to your rescue?
Who really saves the day?
When you lonely or lost
Who shows you the way?

Do they wear a cape?
Invincible and super-strong?
If you think that makes a hero
In reality- you are wrong!

They're just ordinary people
Choosing to help others
Showing selflessness and kindness
They are our sisters and our brothers

Not all are rich and famous,
Magic makers with superpowers.
Time cannot be shortened,
Daily devotion lasts for hours.

There is no 'main hero',
Who saves the world alone
Telepathically sensing danger
They are alerted by phone.

So thankful for these heroes,
No cape, but scrubs or uniform
Making amazing differences to lives,
Being ' super and special' is their norm.

The Strongest Impact

Thank you to everyone
Who I've met in my life,
Through blood, work and socialising
Both in happiness, and times of strife.

Whether still present and consistent
Or in the past - with me no longer,
If we've connected emotionally,
Your impact on me lasts stronger.

Learning from the inspirational,
How to turn my into dreams reality.
From the toxic and devious
About the kind of person *I* want to be.

So grateful for the kind-hearted
Life's cheerleaders, I look forward to see
Those who don't criticise or patronise
But have encouraged and supported me.

Both your words and actions
Make everything true and real
Although messages can be redacted
I won't forget the way you made me feel.

ABOUT THE AUTHOR

Zowie Norris is thrilled to share her first poetry anthology and second published book. She has two poems published in international magazines and posts a weekly poem on her social media author pages. 'Barb the Bird of Hope' her first Children's book, was published in June 2021. It was at this time, that she started sharing weekly poems, rekindling her passion for writing poetry.

Zowie studied English and teaching at Bretton Hall College, West Yorkshire, England, graduating in 1998. Since then, she has shared her passion for creative writing with the pupils in six different primary schools in South Yorkshire, as a teacher and educational leader for the last twenty-five years.

Family is important to Zowie, who lives with her husband James and two daughters, Phoebe and Jasmine. The loss of her beloved mother, and managing anxieties around the pandemic, highlighted the importance of family, gratitude, helping others, having hope and a positive mindset.

You can follow Zowie and her poetry writing on her social media pages.

https://www.facebook.com/zowienorrisauthor

https://www.instagram.com/zowie_norris_author

https://www.Twitter.com@ZowieNorris

@barbthebirdofhope22

If you have enjoyed my poetry, review on Amazon
and/or Goodreads. Your support is always appreciated.

Printed in Great Britain
by Amazon

25934282R00046